DRAWN TOGETHER

Relationships Lampooned, Harpooned & Cartooned

Edited by
Nicole Hollander, Skip Morrow and Ron Wolin
for The Cartoonists Guild

CROWN PUBLISHERS, INC.

NEW YORK

ALSO SPONSORED BY THE CARTOONISTS GUILD

The Art in Cartooning

Animals Animals Animals

Copyright © 1983 by The Cartoonists Guild, Inc.

Published by Crown Publishers, Inc., One Park Avenue, New York, New York 10016 and simultaneously in Canada by General Publishing Company Limited

Manufactured in the United States of America

Library of Congress Cataloging in Publication Data

Drawn together.

  1. Sex customs—Caricatures and cartoons. 2. American wit and humor, Pictorial. I. Hollander, Nicole. II. Morrow, Skip. III. Wolin, Ron. IV. Cartoonists Guild.
NC1426.D72 1983   741.5'973   83-7734

ISBN 0-517-55055-5

10 9 8 7 6 5 4 3 2 1

First Edition

INTRODUCTION

Browsing through the personals section of almost any large urban newspaper, one finds considerable column inches devoted to a craving for some sort of relationship. Surely this is a sign of the times, as are the vast number of books extant on numerous aspects of emotional growth, how-to sex manuals, and documentations of conquests along the path to happiness—to say nothing of resort weekends for swingers, computer dating and singles bars. There is a visceral yearning for The Relationship. It's become serious, big business.

It was not always so. Locating a partner used to be a practical matter. Often it was not even handled by the people involved. Arranged marriages had more to do with family alliances, economics and the assurance of progeny for the sake of inheritance than considerations of chemistry and the heart. For thousands of years, up to our own century, the custom of the dowry dominated the process of marrying. North America was settled in part by mail-order brides and mothers responding to an early version of Help Wanted ads.

We're doing things somewhat differently these days:

I'M PART SWISS ARMY KNIFE, part French perfume. 5'4", 115, 34. Well traveled (still curious). I'm ready for a lasting relationship with secure, professional man of slightly wild mind, humanitarian spirit and tender, educated hands; a nonsmoker, physically fit. Photo please.

TIRED OF KISSING FROGS? Ready to meet your prince? Attorney, 38, seeks warm, loving counterpart, with sense of humor, willing to travel, love and learn together.

Between then and now was the heyday of "The Battle of the Sexes" and most of the cartoons we're used to seeing about relationships reflect that point of view. The collection at hand goes beyond the strictly adversarial in the same way as the dumb blond and nagging mother-in-law clichés have been toppled from their once impregnable positions in the world of humor. The old stuff is unfortunately still with us, but now we have other things to look at and think about.

You may be assuming that the relationships depicted are solely what happen between men and women seeking romance. That's part of it, but so is what happens between men and men, women and women, parents and kids, kids and kids, people and society, everyone and pets—whether reading the paper at the breakfast table, strolling down the street or dealing with the myriad possibilities of the bedroom. And the experiences include everything from betrayal, boredom, bitterness and jealousy to attraction, independence, and ecstasy.

Drawn Together presents the work of 146 cartoon and comic artists from the 1890s to 1980s, in more than 325 drawings—single panels, comic strips, editorial cartoons and multipage continuities. Eleven countries are represented, and there are more works by women cartoonists than in any previous anthology of this scale. Never before have so many diverse artists and styles been surveyed in a collection commenting on a single theme.

The 1980s have witnessed a virtual explosion of interest in cartoon books. A recent study published by the Cartoonists Guild indicated a record 143 such books published in the United States and Canada during 1982—a twenty percent increase over 1981, and almost three times as many as in 1980. On the *New York Times* weekly Trade Paperback Best Seller List in 1982 the largest category was cartoon and comic art, with a total of twenty different titles appearing between January and December. During one period, nine out of the fifteen on the list were cartoon collections, and on any given Sunday there were never less than four. Two cartoon books showed up on the Hardcover Non-Fiction List the same year, one for fifty consecutive weeks. Seven cartoon books were tapped as book club selections.

Paralleling this trend in publishing has been the art world's intensely renewed interest in drawing as a medium, with a dramatic rise in the number of exhibitions, books, catalogs and articles. Part of this attention has focused on cartoon and comic art as a dynamic form of drawing and a natural means of expressing social and political concerns. This reflects the move away from nonrepresentational and abstract art to the figurative mode and all that it implies about gesture, characterization and content, which are at the core of cartoon and comic art. In addition, there are museums and galleries dedicated to this form in the United States, Canada and Europe.

Cartooning can be done spontaneously, quickly and inexpensively. Its informality and accessibility have made it a democratic and ubiquitous medium. People have grown up with it and feel comfortable around it. So, we asked ourselves, what could be more natural than to explore a phenomenon everyone is interested in, using an art form everyone enjoys?

Without further ado, we present for your instant gratification and time-released relief—*Drawn Together: Relationships Lampooned, Harpooned & Cartooned.*

New York, May 1983

Ron Wolin
Executive Director, Cartoonists Guild

FRANK MODELL

*"I've been dying to get you two together. You're the two most amusing men
I've ever met."*

5

M. K. BROWN

1976

G. B. TRUDEAU

1978

MICHAEL C. WITTE

MISS YOUR TERN

1981

WALTER GALLUP

1981

MIKE PETERS

MOOD MUSIC

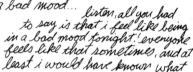

CLAIRE BRETÉCHER

1980   HOWARD MARGULIES

*"When I say 'I love you,' I mean, 'I really love you!' . . .
I don't think you understand . . . I mean, 'love you! Really!' . . .
Maybe you don't fully comprehend . . . 'I really love you!' . . ."*

1971   WILLIAM STEIG

1970 MARVIN TANNENBERG

"This is a recording—but the person who made the recording is a warm, compassionate human being."

CHARLES ADDAMS

"You're seeing another woman, aren't you, Robert?"

JAMES THURBER

"All right, have it your way—you heard a seal bark."

WHITNEY DARROW, JR.

"Miss! Oh, Miss! For God's sake, stop!"

Young ladies, prior to marriage, must stay ready.

Take it easy with the after-shave.

Introduce some fresh ideas into your sex life.

CONTINUED

Grow together.

There is much loose talk
going around about
polygamy.
Ignore it.

For better
or for worse,
support your spouse.

In the ideal marriage both partners are vulnerable.

Take time to fall in love again.

Remember: Some people are not marriageable.

BOOTH

GEORGE BOOTH

HELEN E. HOKINSON

"We planned Chester very carefully."

ca. 1970   AL HIRSCHFELD

GEORGE AND IRA GERSHWIN

KRAZY KAT

GEORGE HERRIMAN

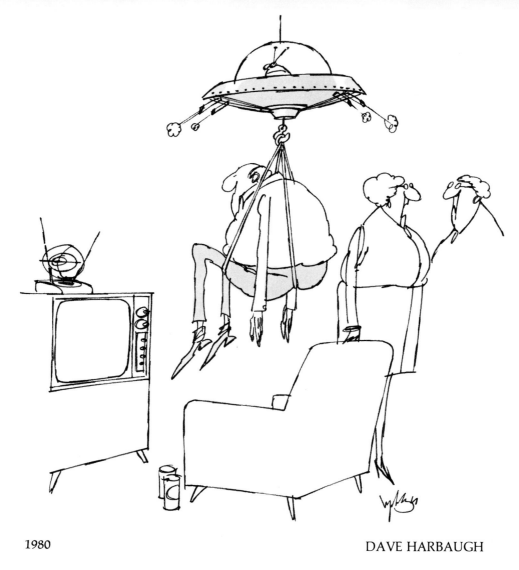

1980

DAVE HARBAUGH

"They asked permission to take some inert material back to Venus. . . ."

1979 M. K. BROWN

"So then Howard came along. He was Canadian, but couldn't make
a nest to save his soul, poor thing. But we had a lot of laughs,
Howard and I. I remember one time . . ."

1982 SKIP MORROW

GEORGE PRICE

"We'll call you back after nine. We're in the middle of the Family Hour."

All right mother, I'm going to count up to three and I want you to come out with your hands above your head.

1966   JOHN GLASHAN

STINE

1981   RICHARD STINE

The Causes of Lesbianism:

a simple guide in pictures.....
by Jo Nesbitt

biologically determined?

Unpleasant experience with male at an impressionable age

pleasant experience with female at an impressionable age

Disappointed wife transfers affection to Daughter.....

mother's fault

The Distant Father.....

father's fault

JO NESBITT

PETER ARNO

"Wake up, you mutt! We're getting married today."

WILLIAM HAMILTON

"Tell me, Sara, why does your young man keep calling your mother 'man'?"

1971

WILLIAM STEIG

SYD HOFF

"Can't you see by now, Bernard Levin, that it's all over between us?"

1981   JOHN TROY

"My only regret is I had to give up fishing."

1980

CHARLES M. SCHULZ

1953   VIRGIL PARTCH

"Are you <u>always</u> this inhibited, Mr. Filstrup?"

1982   FERENC SAJDIK

1968   DAVID LEVINE

THE TICKET

GEORGE BOOTH

"Attention, everyone! Here comes Poppa, and we're going to drive dull care away! It's quips and cranks and wanton wiles, nods and becks and wreathed smiles."

FRANK MODELL

*"She had the Jordache look, and he had the
Ralph Lauren look, and they collided."*

JAMES THURBER

"Why, I never dreamed your union had been blessed with issue!"

1982

NICOLE HOLLANDER

1980   RICHARD FIALA

"Now click your heels three times and say 'There's no such thing as a perfect relationship.'"

1982   ROLAND MICHAUD

"All he ever thinks about is you know what."

TRINA ROBBINS

The March Of Men

1981   DAVE LESTER

1979   NICOLE HOLLANDER

1978   DON DOUGHERTY

38

1977

BILL BASSO

*"Al, you're a sweetheart. Listen, gotta run. Call me Friday for a quick bite.
Beautiful! Love to Fern and the kids. Ciao!"*

39

PETER ARNO

*"It's quite late, dear, and I'm tired. Would you mind
starting your summation?"*

HELEN E. HOKINSON

"*After hearing Colonel Morgan, I'm sure all of us have overcome
any fear we may have had of Japan.*"

SYD HOFF

"*Miss Green, how would you like never having to worry
about the price of meat for the rest of your life?*"

1980

ON PARENT'S DAY
"Puh-leeze, Mummy, nobody wants to hear about Coke, Acapulco, or Fleetwood Mac."

LIFE WITH ROBINSON

1978

JERRY ROBINSON

SYLVIA

1981

NICOLE HOLLANDER

PEANUTS

1981

CHARLES M. SCHULZ

1

2

3

4

5

6

7

8

SAM COBEAN

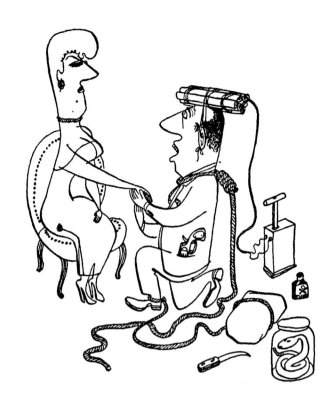

1953   VIRGIL PARTCH

"If . . . if it's 'no,' I'll understand."

1982   SKIP MORROW

LOVE AT FIRST SIGHT

1937   H. T. WEBSTER

1975   JERZY FLISAK

HELEN E. HOKINSON

"You'd think George and Ella would try to patch things up for the children's sake."

PATIENCE AND SARAH

1981

JAN ELIOT

1982

HEATHER McADAMS

Mr. and Ms.
created, written & drawn by MICHAEL SIPORIN ©1981

SLOW DOWN! YOU'RE DRIVING LIKE SOME KIND OF **MANIAC!**

YOU'LL DO **ANYTHING** TO AVOID SEEING MY FAMILY... **INCLUDING** SUICIDE!

DON'T TELL **ME** HOW TO DRIVE!

...AND AS FOR YOUR PARENTS... I DON'T THINK THEY LIKE ME... ...I **REALLY** DON'T!!!

THE LIGHT CHANGED!

I GET THE DISTINCT IMPRESSION THAT THE **ONLY** THING ON THEIR HOT **LITTLE** MINDS IS **WHEN** ARE WE GOING TO **MAKE IT LEGAL?**

THAT IS IN **YOUR** HEAD, MY DEAR!

ON THE OTHER HAND, WHY SHOULD THEY FEEL COMFORTABLE WITH OUR RELATIONSHIP? THEY DON'T UNDERSTAND IT....AND THERE **ARE** TIMES WHEN I FEEL **LIKEWISE!** WATCH OUT FOR THOSE PEOPLE!!

I SEE THEM!!

LOOK....THEY DON'T KNOW **HOW** TO DEAL WITH YOU! YOU'RE NOT A **SON-IN-LAW** ....**OR** A **BOYFRIEND!**

....OR A **GIGOLO!**... OR A **SEDUCER!**... AS **THEY** PREFER TO **SUSPECT!**

THAT LIGHT WAS **RED!**

WILL YOU **STOP** GIVING ME DIRECTIONS?!!

1980

MICHAEL SIPORIN

1971   GLENN BERNHARDT

"I don't like this 'A' in sex education."

1953   J. R. WILLIAMS

LIFE'S DARKEST MOMENT

1941

H. T. WEBSTER

MOMMA

1979

MELL LAZARUS

THE FAMILY AT THE SEASHORE

ca. 1910

HEINRICH KLEY

CRITICISM/SELF-CRITICISM SECTION

ANSWER & DISCUSS THE FOLLOWING QUESTIONS:

1) IS THIS CARTOON FUNNY?
2) IS IT ACTUALLY MAKING FUN OF OPPRESSION?
3) WHAT IS ITS "POINT"?
4) WHO **IS** MORE OPPRESSED?
5) EXPLAIN OTHER WAYS THE RULING CLASS IS TRICKY.
6) IS DAVID ROCKEFELLER THE HEAD OF THE RULING CLASS?
7) WOULD DAVID ROCKEFELLER FIND THIS CARTOON FUNNY?

1979   JAY KINNEY

FOR BETTER OR FOR WORSE

1980   LYNN JOHNSTON

DOONESBURY

1976

G. B. TRUDEAU

1979

FANNY TRIBBLE

GEORGE PRICE

"No, no! The day the earth stood still was in May. We weren't married till June."

SYD HOFF

"Myrtle, I just had to see you."

MARY PETTY

"Which one is the love potion?"

WINSOR McCAY

1899   CHARLES DANA GIBSON

RIVAL BEAUTIES

WHITNEY DARROW, JR.

"It's some radio survey, Ma'am. They want to know if you're happy."

1976   WILLIAM HAMILTON

"Excuse me, Nancy—this isn't the one incapable of sustaining personal relationships, is it?"

THE BOAT THAT DARE NOT SPEAK IT'S NAME

1978   RICHARD FIALA

CHARLES ADDAMS

"Darling!"

Men March On

Panel 1:
Hey you want to join our Men's group Eric?

I don't want to join some nambi-pambi group for men!

Panel 2:
Look its not like that. Feminists are always telling us to go form a group. In otherwords we go and talk behind their backs.

Yah, I see it makes it sort of legal doesn't it. Great idea Tony!

Panel 3:
BROTHER be strong.

Yah Brother, you too but get away from me.

By Dave Lester 79

1979   DAVE LESTER

DR. SCHWARTZ MEETS RICK'S FANTASY-GIRL, DARLEEN

1982   FRANK COLLYER

SORRY IF I WOKE YOU MR. JONES... IT'S FOR YOUR **NEW** ROOMMATE!

5E
JONES
SCHWARTZ

Mr. and Ms.

created, written & drawn by MICHAEL SIPORIN
©1981

IT'S FOR YOU... LOOKS LIKE A CHECKBOOK.... DID YOU PRINT **THIS** ADDRESS ON THEM?

NO....I JUST HAD THEM SENT HERE.....WHY? DOES **THAT** BOTHER YOU?

I GUESS IT DOES!

WHAT DO YOU MEAN?

THIS DOESN'T SEEM TO BE DEVELOPING INTO A STABLE PERMANENT-TYPE RELATIONSHIP!

BUT WE'VE BEEN TOGETHER FOR **MORE** THAN 2½ WEEKS!

I GUESS I WANT SOMETHING ...MORE SUBSTANTIAL..... ... A COMMITMENT... SOMETHING **MORE** LONG TERM!

THAT'S FINE BY ME!... I'D **LIKE** TO SETTLE IN... BRING OVER MY PHILODENDRON..... AND MY GILA MONSTER!!!

JUST A MINUTE! DON'T TAKE ADVANTAGE OF THE SITUATION!

WHAT THE HELL... DOES **THAT** MEAN?

DON'T START PUTTING PRESSURE ON ME!!

REMEMBER! THE LEASE IS IN **MY** NAME!!!

SCREW YOU! I'M GOING!

I BETTER CALL MY SHRINK... **BUT FIRST**, I'LL TAKE **HER** NAME OFF THE DOOR!

SLAM

1981

MICHAEL SIPORIN

FRANK MODELL

"What a coincidence! I couldn't help noticing you're reading a book I was thinking of reading myself."

1950   CHARLES ADDAMS

1979   NICOLE HOLLANDER   65

POGO

A REIGN OF RAIN

CONTINUED

1969

WALT KELLY

GARFIELD

WHAT'S THAT YOU SAY, LITTLE FELLA?

OH, VERY WELL. I'LL HOLD YOU

POOKY NEEDS ME

JIM DAVIS

7-13

© 1982 United Feature Syndicate, Inc.

1982   JIM DAVIS

1982   FERENC SAJDIK

"Everybody has somebody. Only I am married."

1974   DON OREHEK

"Would you guys mind if I slept alone for a change?"

70

ONE EVENING IN A BATHTUB

DON MARTIN

1978 ARNOLDO FRANCHIONI

"Your cubicle or mine?"

1944   BILL MAULDIN

"Why th' hell couldn't you have been born
a beautiful woman?"

1981   MIKE PETERS

HARLEY SCHWADRON

"At a party, Irwin, why do you insist on labeling everyone?"

1979   LYNDA BARRY

CLAUDE SMITH

"Well, now that the children have all grown up, I guess I'll pull up a chair."

SKIPPY

1927

PERCY CROSBY

PEANUTS

1980

CHARLES M. SCHULZ

MOMMA

1978

MELL LAZARUS

FOR BETTER OR FOR WORSE

1980

LYNN JOHNSTON

CATHY

1982

CATHY GUISEWITE

1944

SGT. GEORGE BAKER

1978

RICK MEYEROWITZ

"You put your shirt on over your parrot again."

1968

DON OREHEK

"Before we finish up, Hank, I'd like to say that it's been a real pleasure working with you."

79

1979

MARK BEYER

JAMES STEVENSON

"But I did get my act together. This is my act."

GEORGE BOOTH

"I've got an idea for a story: Gus and Ethel live on Long Island, on the North Shore. He works sixteen hours a day writing fiction. Ethel never goes out, never does anything except fix Gus sandwiches, and in the end she becomes a nympho-lesbo-killer-whore. Here's your sandwich."

PETER ARNO

"Armbruster here has what I think is a marvelous suggestion."

83

1981

CLEM SCALZITTI

SYD HOFF

"As if there aren't enough of us to worry about."

1981   MARTHA CAMPBELL

"Mrs. Horton, could you stop by school today?"

1979   JOSEPH DAWES

HOWARD CRUSE

1980   JARED LEE

"I've never been with a woman before. Would you mind saying baa baa?"

1981   WILLIAM HAEFELI

ELLIOT'S FATHER ONLY TOOK WORKING VACATIONS

HEY, WHOZZAT?

THAT'S SHIRE'S FRIEND FRED.... NO, HIS NAME'S SAM, I THINK..

IF HE SEES ME, WE MAY HAVE TO MAINTAIN EYE CONTACT FOR THE WHOLE BLOCK...

SO, INTO EVASIVE ACTION. LOOK DOWN AT THE GROUND..

...SWEEP CASUALY TO THE RIGHT...

...NOW THE LEFT...

...AND UP!

OH, HI SAM!

UH HI..!

SAM?...

I'VE GOT TO STOP INVESTING SO MUCH ENERGY IN MY PERSONAL RELATIONSHIPS...

1981

MATT FREEDMAN

88

1968   AL HIRSCHFELD

WALTER MATTHAU AND JACK LEMMON IN "THE ODD COUPLE"

1982   SKIP MORROW

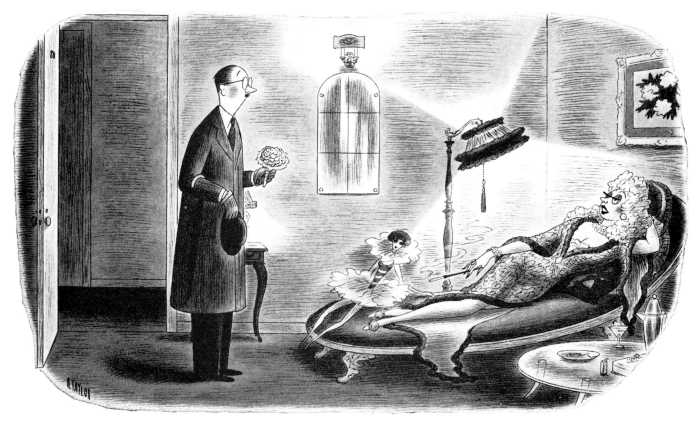

RICHARD TAYLOR

"Mr. Coombes, I'm afraid you and I don't speak the same language."

1965

JEAN-JACQUES SEMPÉ

All You Need Is LOVE

1980

DAVE LESTER

STINE

1980

RICHARD STIN

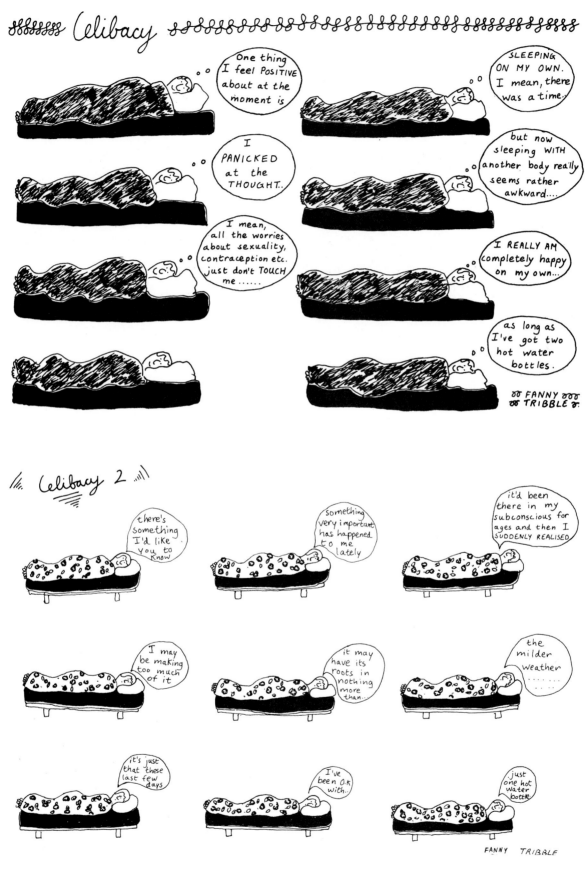

1925

H. T. WEBSTER

FRANK MODELL

"Your friend is more than welcome, dear, but we just want
you to know that your father and I didn't do anything funny
till after we were married."

CHARLES ADDAMS

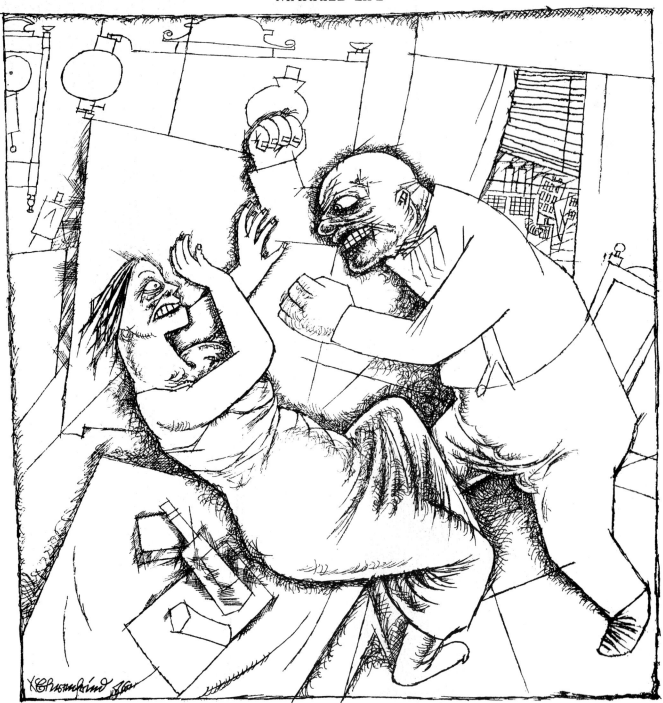

1915

GEORGE GROSZ

1981

RICHARD STINE

1942 WILLIAM STEIG

PEOPLE ARE NO DAMN GOOD

JAMES THURBER

'Well, who made the magic go out of our marriage—you or me?

FRANK MODELL

"Will you kindly remove that bird when I'm talking to you?"

WELL, GEORGE BUNGLE, AT LAST WE HAVE SOMEONE LIVING NEXTDOOR TO US WHO LOOKS AT THE NEIGHBOR PROBLEM AS SENSIBLY AS WE DO.

YES SUH! HE'S GREAT! TO HIM NEIGHBORS ARE MERELY POISON IVY ON THE PATH OF LIFE. HE'S A SMART GUY.

AJAX, AREN'T THOSE BUNGLES NICE! SHE DIDN'T MINCE WORDS IN LETTING ME KNOW SHE CONSIDERS NEIGHBORS TRASH.

HE'S THE MOST BROADMINDED MAN I EVER TALKED WITH ON THIS NEIGHBOR THING FOR ONCE WE'RE LIVING NEXTDOOR TO PEOPLE TOO SMART TO SNEER AT A MAN WHO KNOWS NEIGHBORS AND KNOWS NOTHING GOOD ABOUT 'EM.

1928   HARRY J. TUTHILL   99

MOTHER-IN-LAW BLUES

CLAIRE BRETÉCHER

1953   VIRGIL PARTCH

"Watch it . . . Mother's going to land on you for being late for dinner."

THE THRILL THAT COMES ONCE IN A LIFETIME

NEWLYWEDS FIRST BREAKFAST

DARLING, THIS TOAST IS MARVELOUS. NEVER ATE BETTER TOAST IN MY LIFE. DON'T TELL ME YOU CAN'T COOK. YOU'RE A WIZARD.

1948   H. T. WEBSTER

HELEN E. HOKINSON

"I've put you next to a man who may or may not be dangerous."

WHITNEY DARROW, JR.

*"But I want you to know, Albert, that if
I were going to marry someone like you,
it would certainly be you."*

ca. 1940   GARDNER REA

*"If it weren't for your absurd modesty, Mrs. Esterhazy,
we could rig up some sort of tent."*

1939   J. R. WILLIAMS

1982

MATT FREEDMAN

TON SMITS

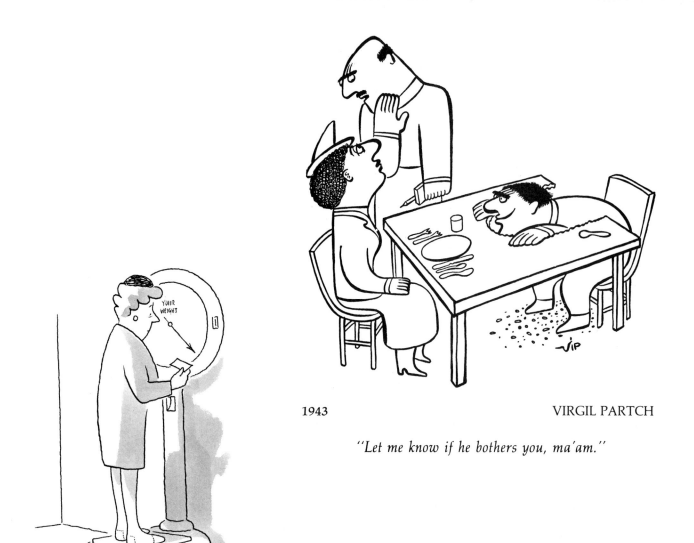

1943   VIRGIL PARTCH

"Let me know if he bothers you, ma'am."

1979   CHON DAY

"You weigh 132 pounds and your feet are cold."

1980   JACK MARKOW

"May I inject a discordant note?"

106

GLUYAS WILLIAMS

RACONTEURS

"James and Cornelia don't like me to run on about the family, but, goodness me, I can't see any reason for being proud of an ancestor just because he was governor—that was James's great-grandfather, over the mantelpiece there— when you know he was a pompous old windbag who probably cheated the poor. My mother told me of one time when our great-aunt Harriet—who, by the way, was no better than she should be—came to visit and . . ."

1981   WILLIAM HOEST

"Please, Lord, let it be that she's just having an affair."

FOR BETTER OR FOR WORSE

1981   LYNN JOHNSTON

1981   LISA ASCHBACHER

1982   JOHN TROY

"Would it help our relationship if I throw it back?"

110

1979

1980   HOWARD MARGULIES

*"Sure, you've got your <u>space</u> and I've got my <u>space</u>. But,
lately, your space is really getting on my nerves!"*

1980   BRUCE COCHRAN

*"It's a terrorist group. They're claiming full
responsibility for your meat loaf."*

1981   LYNDA BARRY

1939

MILT GROSS

RICHARD TAYLOR

"You know the rules, Miss Wigant—no gentlemen
visitors after ten P.M."

PETER ARNO

"What you really want is to marry the girl and settle down.
But you can't, because you're a gorilla."

1979   M. K. BROWN

"Heck, no! We're not crazy! Why? Do we look crazy?"

BEHIND CLAUS DOORS

FROM "CLAUS" BY MICHAEL C. WITTE

FRANK MODELL

"Why do you insist upon finding something good to say about everyone who infuriates me?"

A TOUCH OF CLAUS

MICHAEL C. WITTE

OTTO SOGLOW

1900   CHARLES DANA GIBSON

ACCIDENT TO A YOUNG MAN WITH A WEAK HEART

1944

RUBE GOLDBERG

1

2

3

4

5

6

1982   FERENC SAJDIK

1981   HEATHER McADAMS

1967

BONNIE AND CLYDE

1931

JOHN HELD JR.

"ARE YOU A VIRGIN?" HE ASKED COLDLY

JAMES THURBER

HOUSE AND WOMAN

1902   CHARLES DANA GIBSON

A SUGGESTION FOR ILL-ASSORTED PAIRS

THE PLOT THICKENS

©1980 BILL GRIFFITH

IT WAS A COLD, CLEAR AFTERNOON. CHARLIE BENDIX STIRRED HIS COFFEE WITH A FINGER AS HE CONTEMPLATED HIS NEXT MOVE. THE CAFETERIA WAS EMPTY. IN FACT, IN THAT VAST CAVERN OF TABLES AND CHAIRS, CHARLIE WAS THE ONLY THING STIRRING. THERE WAS NOTHING IN THE PAPER. CHARLIE BENDIX WAS 36. HE STIRRED HIS COFFEE WITH A FINGER AND HE SAID TO HIMSELF:

..MY NAME IS *CHARLIE BENDIX.* I WISH I HAD A *SPOON.*

THEN SHE CAME INTO HIS LIFE. SHE WAS A REPORTER FOR A BIG CITY NEWSPAPER. ON THE SIDE SHE DID "NEON SCULPTURE". SHE LOVED CATS. SHE LOVED DOGS. SHE LOVED PIZZA & SHE LOVED CHARLIE BENDIX.

SHIRLEY? HOW MANY *OIL WELLS* DID YOU SAY YOUR *FATHER* OWNS??

I DON'T KNOW HOW *MANY*..HE HAS *FOURTY-FOUR FIELDS*.. --HE WANTS TO *MEET* YOU...

TEXAS WAS ALIEN TO CHARLIE. HE MISSED THE OCEAN...HE DIDN'T LIKE COWBOY HATS. HE DIDN'T LIKE LONE STAR BEER. HE DIDN'T LIKE THE WIDE, OPEN SPACES. AND HE DIDN'T LIKE LESTER.

H'LO THERE, OL' *BUDDY!!*

CHARLIE, I WANT YOU TO MEET MY *OLD BOYFRIEND, LESTER.* AND MY *FATHER*.. ..AND MY *AUNT NORLEEN*.. AND *COUSIN ANNIE* AND..

NICE *COW-BOY HAT,* LESTER..

LESTER MISTOOK CHARLIE'S DEFERENCE FOR FRIENDSHIP. CHARLIE MARRIED SHIRLEY. THEN ONE DAY:

MY LIFE'S NO BOWL OF *CHERRIES* EITHER, LESTER..

I NEVER TOLD THIS TO *NO ONE,* CHARLIE..BUT *SHIRLEY* AND *ME*.. SHE DON'T *KNOW* THIS..WELL, WE GOT A *KID!!*

CHARLIE MISTOOK LESTER'S HOSTILITY FOR PATHOS. HE RELATED AN INCIDENT FROM HIS PAST.

IT WAS AFTER THE *PLANE CRASH* THAT I TURNED TO *GAMBLING*..

ACTUALLY, CHARLIE WAS LYING. IT WAS HIS 2 YEARS IN THE PRIESTHOOD THAT LED HIM TO THE THE CRAPS TABLE.

MOTEL RULES

1980

BILL GRIFFITH

125

WILLIAM HAMILTON

*"You know what I bet it is? I bet we're breaking up but
we just don't realize it yet."*

ELDON DEDINI

*"Round up the kids, Helen, I've just decided
to spend some time with them."*

JAMES STEVENSON

"O.K. So when we have a party, we won't ask them."

1966   JOHN GLASHAN

ca. 1910   HEINRICH KLEY

CAUGHT IN THE ACT

AT HOME

1922

GEORGE GROSZ

1919

GEORGE HERRIMAN

1971

WILLIAM STEIG

ROBERT DAY

"Well, then, how about Friday evening?"

1981

MATT FREEDMAN

DOONESBURY

1977 G. B. TRUDEAU

1982 ALAN BARAL

"Why can't it be like it was before? . . . When we didn't know one another."

SAM COBEAN

1978   JERRY ROBINSON

1979   RANDALL MAXSON

WOMEN CAN'T REALLY UNDERSTAND MEN'S BODIES.

A MAN'S BODY IS MORE MYSTERIOUS THAN A WOMAN'S BECAUSE THE FEMALES REPRODUCTIVE ORGANS ARE INSIDE HER.

THEREFORE, SHE UNDERSTANDS AND RELATES TO THEM AS A PART OF HERSELF.

WHEREAS, A MAN'S REPRODUCTIVE ORGANS ARE OBVIOUS APPENDAGES.

...A CONFUSING SITUATION SINCE THERE IS NO VISIBLE DIFFERENCE BETWEEN HIS GENITALS AND ANY OTHER UNDESIRABLE GROWTH.

I MEAN... IS IT REALLY A PEE-PEE? OR IS IT A WART? WHO CAN TELL?

1977

SHARY FLENNIKEN

PETER ARNO

"See, darling, I told you we couldn't have a Platonic friendship."

GEORGE PRICE

"Will you be right home after the peccadillo?"

1957

CHARLES ADDAMS

139

A HANDY MAN AROUND THE HOUSE

1923   CLARE BRIGGS

HELEN E. HOKINSON

*"I insist! After all, summoning four ghosts
from the past was my idea."*

WHITNEY DARROW, JR.

"The gentleman wants to know if you'd care to join him in a little argument."

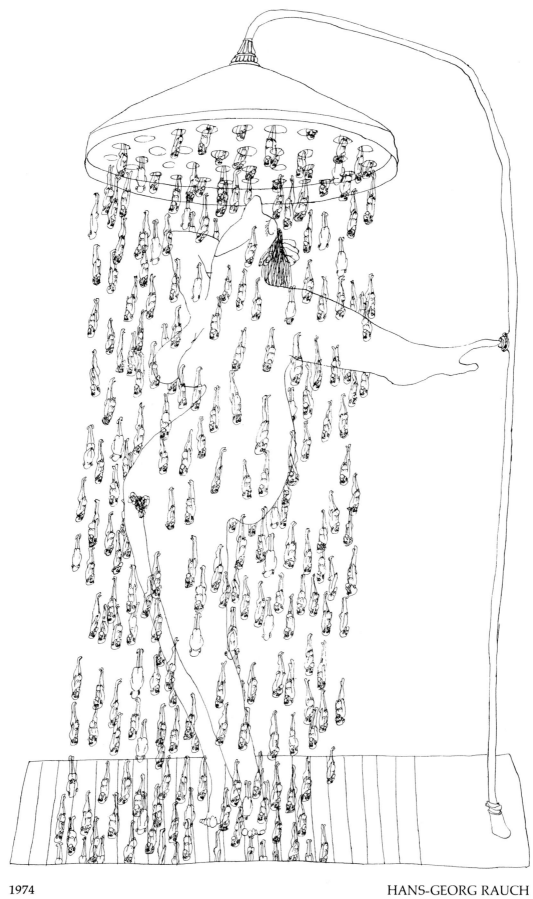

1974

HANS-GEORG RAUCH

142

On Fridays Emblus played the flute;
The bird now joined him on a lute.

The top of the zagava tree
Was frequently where they had tea.

1975

EDWARD GOREY

1979   RICK MEYEROWITZ

"I told her what you said and she said yes, she would go with you to your hotel and yes, you could put your face between her breasts and she said a price could be arranged later and she said not to tell you she's a man."

1980

LYNDA BARRY

1982

STROP

1981   SAUNDRA BENAT

1978   RICHARD FIALA

"It's my parents. Quick, help me think of something heterosexual to say."

DO YOU KNOW DEAR - I THINK LITTLE ARCHIBALD IS GOING TO BE AN ARTIST JUST LIKE HIS DADDY-- HE JUST SITS AND DRAWS ALL THE WHOLE TIME

OH THAT REMINDS ME DEAR--GWENNY HAS SHOWN SUCH A TALENT FOR MUSIC- SHE PLAYS REMARKABLY WELL FOR A CHILD OF SIX- HER UNCLE IS A MUSICIAN YOU KNOW AND .WE THINK—

ARCHIBALD IS NEVER SO HAPPY AS WHEN HE HAS A PENCIL AND PAPER--IT'S REALLY REMARK'BLE THAT CHILD'S IMAGINATION-- WE'RE SAVING ALL HIS WORK FOR FUTURE YEARS- WE THINK HE WILL ——

GWENNY IS ONLY SIX, YOU KNOW BUT PLAYS LIKE A CHILD OF SEVEN- HER TEACHER (WE HAVE ENGAGED THE VERY BEST) HER TEACHER SAYS SHE HAS NEVER IN ALL HER EXPERIENCE SEEN A CHILD OF THAT AGE, WITH SUCH A GRASP OF MUSIC—

OH DEAR ALICE IS SO TIRING! ALWAYS BORING PEOPLE ABOUT GWENNY! WHY THE CHILD HAS NO MORE TALENT FOR MUSIC THAN A LUMP OF MUD

GRACIE IS SO AMUSING AND BORING! SHE REALLY THINKS THAT POOR SIMP OF A KID HAS TALENT! ABOUT AS MUCH TALENT AS MY BIG TOE!

1925

CLARE BRIGGS

WINSOR McCAY

MARY PETTY

"The Indians had him completely at bay. He saved his last shot for
your Great-Great-Great Aunt Fanny."

1930   H. T. WEBSTER

ANATOL KOVARSKY

1963   JERRY ROBINSON

ca. 1958   TON SMITS

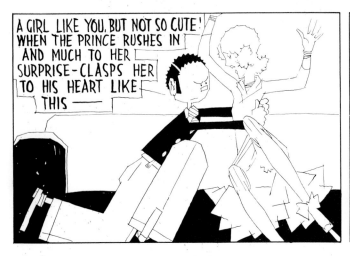

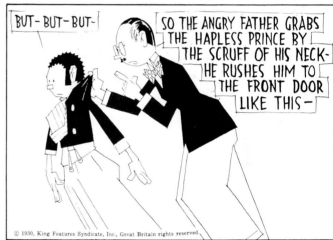

1930

JOHN HELD JR.

1976

G. B. TRUDEAU

1976   HARLEY SCHWADRON

*"In all our 23 years of marriage, Albert, what do you consider
the outstanding newspaper headline?"*

1980   LEN HERMAN

PATIENCE AND SARAH

1982

JAN ELIOT

FOR BETTER OR FOR WORSE

1980

LYNN JOHNSTON

WEE PALS

1978

MORRIE TURNER

PEANUTS

1981   CHARLES M. SCHULZ

SKIPPY

1927   PERCY CROSBY

ELDON DEDINI

"Every once in a while I write home for a little money.
It keeps them from worrying."

1973   JOHN RUGE

"Mr. Hobart, I'd like to pick your brains about carrots."

GLUYAS WILLIAMS

RACONTEURS

"Well, good night again—this time we really are off. You know, Wallace scolds me. He says I never think of things I want to say until I have my wraps on and have said good night. Just last evening we got roped in for bridge at the Northrops', and you know how Wallace loathes bridge, though I must say he's a lamb about playing, but anyway I tried to break away early, and we got all ready to go, and . . ."

Over the years I have learned to hate your sensitive face

1966   JOHN GLASHAN

1978   HARLEY SCHWADRON

"Well, then, will you marry me next after Herb?"

1981   FRANK COTHAM

"This rivalry has got to stop, Harold!"

160

A FAIRY STORY

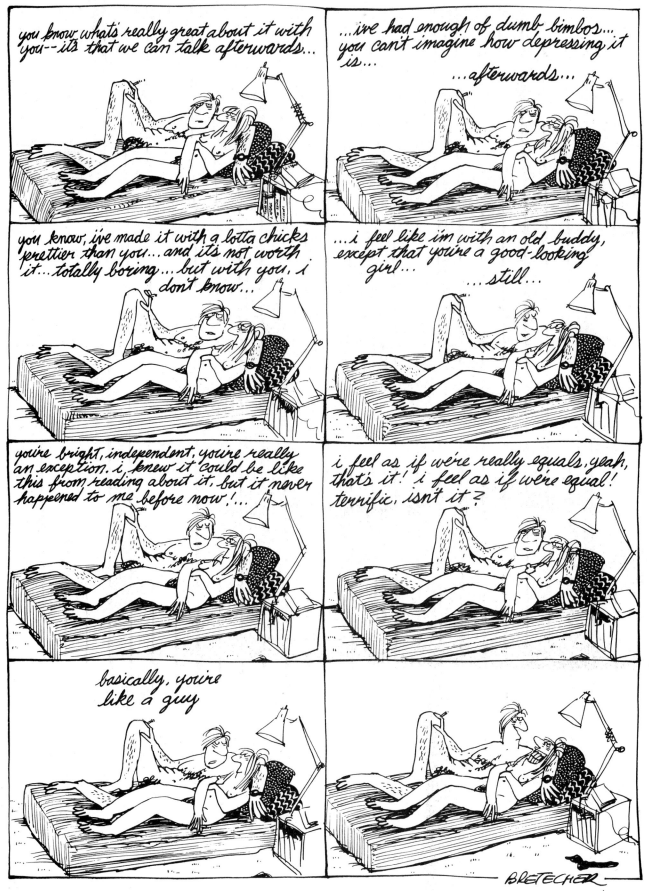

CLAIRE BRETÉCHER

CHARLES ADDAMS

"Now, remember, you can have him as long as you feed him and take good care of him. When you don't, back he goes."

JAMES STEVENSON

"Bertha, will you do me a favor and stop reading those damn 'How to Save Your Marriage' articles?"

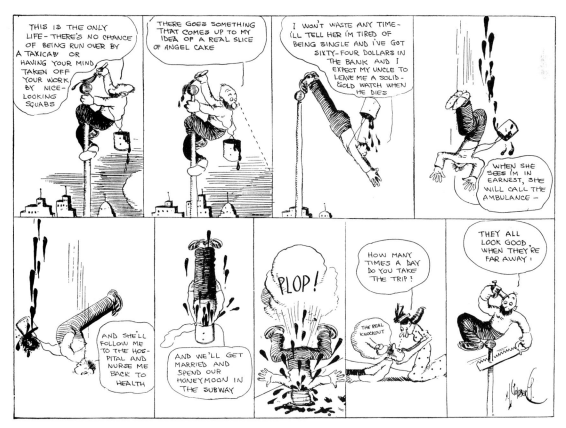

1911

RUBE GOLDBERG

THEY ALL LOOK GOOD WHEN THEY'RE FAR AWAY

1980 REAMER KELLER

"I never did know why they stick their heads in those things."

1981 JERRY MARCUS

"Truth is, I'm not really 'man's best friend,' I'm your best friend."

GARFIELD

WHAT'S SO SPECIAL ABOUT A PET-OWNER RELATIONSHIP, GARFIELD?

COULD IT BE EVERYONE NEEDS SOMEONE TO LORD OVER?

COULD BE

© 1981 United Feature Syndicate, Inc.   JIM DAVIS

BUT WHAT DO **YOU** GET OUT OF IT?

11-13

1981   JIM DAVIS

1979   ED SZEPELAK

*"You are honest, loyal, and extremely
dependable. Your secret ambition is
to outsmart the cat next door."*

1978   DON DOUGHERTY

"Hey! Can't you read?"

AND NOW...
Mary Wilshire presents
MORE Nasty WOMEN'S HUMOR

WOMEN DON'T TALK LIKE THIS!?

WHY DON'T YOU TRY TAKING THESE TO THE 'LAMPOON?

THE YOUNG AND THE INDISCREET

WELL, WANDA I HOPE YOU HEARD WHAT THE POPE HAD TO SAY ABOUT YOUR LIFESTYLE.

YEAH WHUT.

HE SAYS HE JUST CAN NOT CONDONE "CASUAL SEX."

OH REALLY?

AND JUST **WHEN** HAVE YOU EVER KNOWN ME TO TAKE A **CASUAL** ATTITUDE TOWARD SEX?

AGGRESSIVE WOMEN *

HI! WANNA ARM WRESTLE?

I BEG YOUR PARDON?

COME ON— A FEW QUICK ROUNDS

AHH... NO THANKS.

LOSER MAKES BREAKFAST...

AREN'T YOU ASSUMING QUITE A BIT?

I CAN'T COOK, BUT I LIFT WEIGHTS THREE NIGHTS A WEEK...

* PAUL ANTHONY BERNARDO

REMEMBER MURPHY?

POOR BILLY JEAN!

WHAT A DRAG. SHE HANDLED IT SO INTELLIGENTLY, TOO.

WELL, SHE'LL NEVER BREAK **THAT** MURPHY'S LAW AGAIN.

WHICH MURPHY'S LAW IS THAT?

"...NEVER GET INTO BED WITH ANYONE CRAZIER THAN YOU ARE."

HUNH.

166

BEACH BLANKET BINGO

PUNK MOM

1981   MARY WILSHIRE

1966   MARVIN TANNENBERG

*"If you're not deceiving me, how is it that
I never catch you doing anything wrong?"*

1979   MARTHA CAMPBELL

WILLIAM HAMILTON

"Technically, I do love you."

BOAT PEOPLE

1981

MATT FREEDMAN

1982

AREND VAN DAM

1982

NICOLE HOLLANDER

JAMES STEVENSON

"The social fabric is extremely fragile around here."

1

2

1982   JOHN R. CASSADY

*"I practice violin partly to please my mother and partly
to drive my sister up the wall."*

3

4

ca. 1960   TON SMITS

1981   JERRY MARCUS

*"Are you going to believe me, your own flesh
and blood, or some stranger you married?"*

1981

CHARLES M. SCHULZ

1969   DAVID LEVINE

EISENHOWER, KENNEDY, JOHNSON, NIXON, THIEU

1982   RICHARD STINE

CONTINUED

THE SANITARIUM WAS FAR AWAY FROM EVERYTHING — SO PEACEFUL, SO QUIET.

LOOK AT HOW BEAUTIFUL THESE GARDENS ARE, ANJA.

UH HUH

PEOPLE CAME FROM ALL OVER THE WORLD WITH DIFFERENT SICKNESSES. IT WAS EVEN SHOPS HERE... A THEATER... REALLY BEAUTIFUL...

OUR ROOM IS LIKE A LUXURY HOTEL — LOOK AT THIS VIEW.

UH HUH

EACH MORNING NURSES WOULD VISIT TO ANJA.

AND EACH FEW DAYS I TALKED TO THE BIG SPECIALIST AT THE CLINIC.

WELL, WHAT DID THE DOCTOR SAY??

HE TOLD ME YOU'RE DOING FINE... FINE..

JUST RELAX.

I UNDERSTOOD MUCH OF SUCH SICKNESSES, SO I HELPED ALWAYS TO CALM HER DOWN.

LOOK — WE GOT A LETTER FROM HOME TODAY.

WITH A PHOTO OF RICHIEU — LET ME SEE.

HE'S A HANDSOME BOY... JUST LIKE HIS FATHER, YES?

YES.

IN THE EVENINGS WE WENT EITHER TO THE THEATER OR TO DANCE IN THE CAFE.

DID I TELL YOU THE TRAGEDY ABOUT THE PILLOW MY FAMILY LOST AT THE START OF THE 1914 WAR! I WAS SEVEN... WE LIVED TOO CLOSE TO THE BORDER... IT WASN'T SAFE...

I TOLD HER MANY JOKES AND STORIES TO KEEP HER BUSY... ...SO WE TOOK WHAT WE COULD ON A WAGON PULLED BY FOUR HORSES AND WENT TO MY GRANDFATHER'S HOME IN RADOMSKO.

SOMEONE RODE PAST US AND TOLD US THAT WE'D DROPPED A PILLOW A FEW MILES BACK. A GUY TRAVELING TO AMSTOW PICKED IT UP.

IMAGINE — MY FATHER NEVER RODE A HORSE BEFORE... BUT HE UNHITCHED ONE FROM THE WAGON AND RODE TOWARD AMSTOW..

WE WAITED AND WAITED... MOTHER STARTED CRYING: "SURELY HE FELL AND GOT KILLED!" SHE HAD BEGGED HIM TO "LET THE PILLOW GO AND TAKE ALL OUR TROUBLES WITH IT!"

THE HORSE WAS BONY AND DIDN'T HAVE A SADDLE... FINALLY, LATE THAT NIGHT, FATHER RODE BACK WITH THE PILLOW.. ...UNDER HIS BLOODY 'TUCHUS'!...

SO, FATHER GOT HIS PILLOW BACK ...BUT HE COULDN'T SIT DOWN FOR THE REST OF THE WAR!

I LOVE YOU, VLADEK.

AND SHE WAS SO LAUGHING AND SO HAPPY, SO HAPPY, THAT SHE APPROACHED EACH TIME AND KISSED ME, SO HAPPY SHE WAS.

CONTINUED

177

178

MY EYE STARTED SO BLEEDING, I HAD TO RUN OUT TO FIND A DOCTOR IN A DIFFERENT HOSPITAL.

THERE ANOTHER SPE-CIALIST OPERATED RIGHT AWAY! OTHERWISE I COULD HAVE DIED.

SO NOW ITS A GLASS EYE.

HE DID A GOOD JOB, NO? ONE TIME, EVEN, A YOUNG DOCTOR CAME TO MY BED THERE IN THE HOSPITAL....

HE LOOKED WITH A LIGHT A LONG TIME IN MY EYES AND TOLD: 'MR. SPIEGELMAN YOUR LEFT EYE IS PERFECT!..

'...BUT IN YOUR RIGHT EYE IS CATARACTS.'

HE DIDN'T KNOW, OF COURSE, THAT THE LEFT EYE IS GLASS...

AND I DIDN'T TELL ANYTHING TO HIM. I DIDN'T WANT TO MAKE HIM AN EMBARRASSMENT.

UH-HUH- YOU TOLD ME ABOUT THAT.

WELL, IT'S ENOUGH FOR TODAY, YES? I'M TIRED AND I MUST COUNT STILL MY PILLS.

OKAY, GOOD IDEA... MY HAND IS SORE FROM WRITING ALL THIS DOWN.

1981

ART SPIEGELMAN

HELEN E. HOKINSON

"Elizabeth Conner McMeekin, '15?"

"Present. After graduation, I started to take an M.A. at Teachers College, but gave it up to marry Roy McMeekin, Cornell, '12. My husband was only a plant engineer with the telephone company at the time and had not yet become an executive. We lived in Columbus, Ohio, until 1927, when Mr. McMeekin was called to New York, and we built a home in Westchester. I have two children, a girl, Elsie, aged nineteen, and a boy, Donald, aged seventeen. I want to say that I think this Alpha Delta Alpha alumnae picnic is a wonderful idea and that Penny Trowbridge should be congratulated on getting it up. I hope we can get together next summer and repeat it with all the same people."

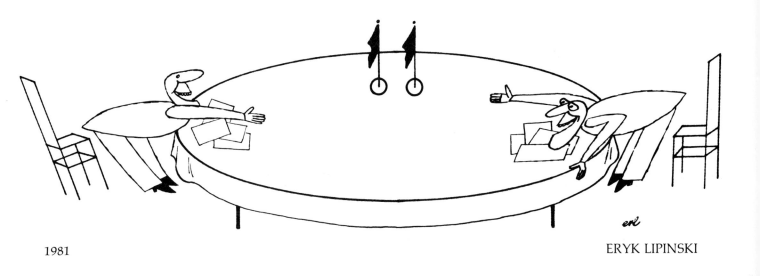

1981

ERYK LIPINSKI

1916

RUBE GOLDBERG

WHEN A RICH MAN SNEEZES, THEY SET IT TO MUSIC

SAUNDRA BENAT

IF ALL WOMEN SECRETLY WANT TO BE RAPED,

IF I HAVEN'T BEEN RAPED,

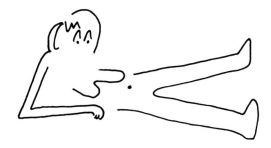

YOU'RE NOT A REAL WOMAN IF YOU DON'T WANT TO BE RAPED.

MAYBE I SECRETLY DON'T WANT TO BE A WOMAN.

BUT SINCE YOU ALWAYS GET WHAT YOU REALLY WANT,

I'VE GOT TO FIND A SHRINK TO HELP ME GET RAPED.

1973

ELLEN LEVINE

183

1982

MORT DRUCKER

1975

BERNARD TANGUAY

PEANUTS

1981

CHARLES M. SCHULZ

1982

MICHAEL DATER

*"And if you ever bump into a sulfur-crested cockatoo name of Fred,
tell him howdy from Wilma. He'll remember."*

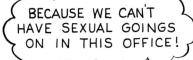

1978

1982

JANIS GOODMAN

1979

JAY KINNEY

GLUYAS WILLIAMS

RACONTEURS

"I hope you won't mind if the girls and I peek in. It's almost like a pilgrimage to us to come back to the rooms where we spent those four golden years. Oh, it does bring it all back so! The Three Musketeers, we called ourselves, and the high jinks that these four walls could tell of! Oh, girls, do you remember the time that . . ."

JAMES THURBER

"Well, I'm disenchanted, too. We're <u>all</u> disenchanted."

DOONESBURY

1976   G. B. TRUDEAU

1979

JO NESBITT

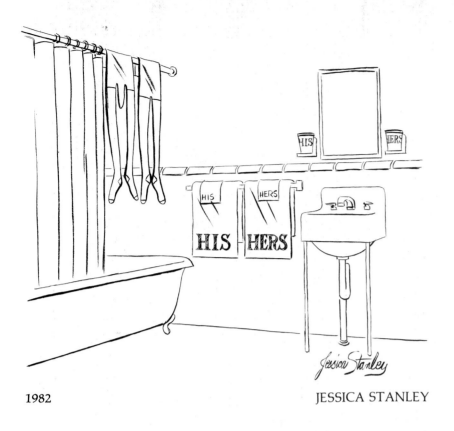

1982

JESSICA STANLEY

VERBENA

1981

PERRY HOWZE

1981   LYNN JOHNSTON

1982   PEARL HILL

*"Living together determines if we should marry, which determines
if we should live together!"*

1978

RICHARD FIALA

"Every time you have an orgasm, I feel like notifying your next of kin."

1982

HEATHER McADAMS

DICK CODOR

DICK CODOR

196

CONTINUED

SHARY FLENNIKEN

1976   RICHARD KIRKMAN

"Water!"

1962   STANLEY STAMATY

"Some day, Dad, this room will be all yours!"

ca. 1956

TON SMITS

1969

WHITNEY DARROW, JR.

"Hey, Ma. How come I'm so plain and you're so fancy?"

"I think it's turning into a boy."

FROM "A TIME FOR INNOCENCE." DRAWINGS BY WHITNEY DARROW, JR.

ANATOL KOVARSKY

*"Pardon me, madam, but I have a feeling
we were meant for each other."*

1981   MIKE KREFFEL

1944   BILL MAULDIN

*"Joe, yestiddy ya saved my life an' I swore I'd pay ya back.
Here's my last pair of dry socks."*

ALBERT KING — JOPO DE POJO

I'LL PLAY THE BLUES FOR YOU

IF YOU'RE DOWN AND OUT
AND YOU FEEL REAL HURT

COME ON OVER
TO THE PLACE WHERE I LIVE

AND ALL YOUR LONELINESS
I'LL TRY TO SOOTHE

I'LL PLAY THE BLUES FOR YOU

DON'T BE AFRAID
COME ON IN

YOU MIGHT RUN ACROSS
SOME OF YOUR OLD FRIENDS

ALL YOUR LONELINESS
I GOTTA SOOTHE

I'LL PLAY THE BLUES FOR YOU

I GOT NO BIG NAME
AND I AIN'T NO BIG STAR

I PLAY THE BLUES FOR YOU
ON MY GUITAR

ALL YOUR LONELINESS I TRY TO SOOTHE
I'LL PLAY THE BLUES FOR YOU

1977

JOOST SWARTE

203

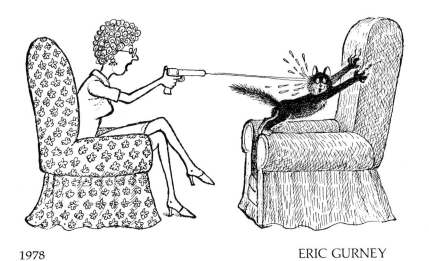

1978   ERIC GURNEY

Patience and firmness are needed to establish
a viable relationship.

1977   WALTER GALLUP

MARMADUKE   *"The hand I bite feeds me."*

1982   BRAD ANDERSON

"He's no trouble. He does what he wants,
and we do what he wants."

GARFIELD

1981

JIM DAVIS

1979

HERB BRAMMEIER, JR.

1972   MARVIN TANNENBERG

". . . Then on the other hand, bup-a-bup, a bup-bup, ba-pup-pup . . ."

1971   BILL BERGERON

1922

GEORGE GROSZ

THE RELATIONSHIP THAT WOULD NOT DIE!!

ON the ROCKS.

part two OF BREAKING UP

YOUR GUIDE TO PAINFUL SEPARATION BY LYNDA BARRY

CRACK!

happy home

"Exactly why couples who hate each other remain together in living hell and call their condition "LOVE" is beyond me."
— Albert Einstein

"Trying to tell someone to leave a relationship that is bad for them is like pissing on the towering inferno." — MIMI POND

FACE IT

ARE YOU REALLY HAPPY??

THERE COMES A TIME IN ALL relationships when you must ask yourself "IS IT WORTH IT?" And as sad as it seems, sometimes the answer is NO! Most often however, the answer to this question is "KINDA" or "SORTA" Take This Easy Test check one

- WHEN I DREAM ABOUT MY BOYFRIEND, HE IS:
  ☐ bringing me flowers
  ☐ trying to kill me with a salami wrapped in the sports page.
- WHEN WE FIGHT, IT IS USUALLY OVER SOMETHING LIKE:
  ☐ major politcal issues
  ☐ issues from the bible
  ☐ how he chews too loud every goddamn time he eats. I can't take it.

THE DIG IS UP BRAND PENCIL

- WHEN I GO TO A PARTY WITH A GIRLFRIEND AND HE STAYS HOME:
  ☐ I drink a small glass of water and sit in a closet away from all other men wishing I were home.
  ☐ I wear my underpants on my head after two drinks and cry when I have to go home.
- THE FIRST THING THAT COMES TO MY MIND WHEN I THINK OF MY RELATIONSHIP IS:
  ☐ seagulls flying free
  ☐ Rats used in scientific experiments

GEE, I GUESS I AM MISERABLE, AND YET I CANNOT LEAVE HIM.

"SO VERY HARD TO GO"

(WHAT are YOU WAITING FOR?)

It is always hard to leave a relationship that is hard to leave. Always, always, always! Usually, unless one of you dies or finds someone else, your relationship can drag on for months, years, YEARS! YEARS! OF bickering, boredom, balding, backbiting, bitching, benality, blaming, brooding, BUNK!

☑ Check the statements that apply to you. (neatness counts)

☐ "But what if I am really happy but I just can't tell right now?"

☐ "But then I'll have to take the bus all the time"

☐ "I think if we are both really commited to making the relationship work....."

☐ "But we look really good together"

☐ "But what if he gets another girlfriend, like, right away?"

☐ "I don't want to hurt him."

☐ ------------------ FILL IN

THE NIGHT YOU CALL IT QUITS

"ITS BEEN ONE HELL OF A NIGHT--- YOU'VE BEEN FIGHTING OVER EVERYTHING. HE WALKED OUT OF THE THEATER BECAUSE YOU WERE CHEWING ICE CUBES AGAIN. YOU SAT IN STONEY SILENCE DURING THE DRIVE HOME AND HOPED HE'D CRASH INTO SOMETHING. BOTH OF YOU SLAMMED THINGS WHILE GETTING READY FOR BED. FINALLY ONE OF YOU SAYS IT.....

I CANT TAKE IT ANYMORE!!

THIS IS IT IM LEAVING! I MEAN IT.

IT DOESN'T MAKE SENSE. WE ARE ALWAYS AT EACH OTHERS THROATS! WE WOULD BE BETTER OFF APART. -RIGHT? -RIGHT?

I MEAN, IT CAN'T WORK OUT - AND BESIDES, YOU'RE PROBABLY SO SICK OF ME YOU WOULDN'T WANT TO TRY TO MAKE IT WORK.

YES I WOULD. LETS TRY

DONT EVER LEAVE ME!

1979   RIP MATTESON

"You knew I was dedicated to fighting the forces of evil when you married me."

1981   LYNDA BARRY

1979

TURHAN SELCUK

1981

ANTONIO ARTUNES

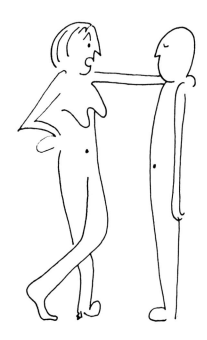

1973   ELLEN LEVINE

"I sometimes wonder if you're the right one for me to be submissive to."

1964   DON OREHEK

"You have no idea how nice it is to have someone to talk to."

1978   RICK MEYEROWITZ

"T. G. I. F."

ARNOLDO FRANCHIONI

1915

GEORGE HERRIMAN

SAM COBEAN

1982

SKIP MORROW

ONE NIGHT I DREAMT I WAS TRAPPED IN ONE OF THOSE GOTHIC ROMANCES BY WOMEN WITH THREE NAMES..

WHAT... A ..."STORY"... MADEMOISELLE...

TRULY UNBELIEVABLE... FAMILY CIRCLE

..NEVER SEEN ANYTHING LIKE IT... MONTGY. ADVERTISER-JOURNAL

..SHE HAS DONE IT AGAIN... EAST IOWA GAZETTE

© 1973/78 LEE MARRS

My Deadly, My Love
GERALDINE POE FITZPUGHIS

WHEN FIRST I GAZED UPON THE FABLED GABLES OF CASTLE FERNLIK, LITTLE DID I ERE SUSPICION WHAT NEFARIOUS DEEDS WOULD SOON ECHO THROUGH ITS DANK CHAMBERS — AND THROUGH MY DRAB, DOWDY LIFE !

CHEEZ. WOTTA DUMP.

BOO !!

AHK!

HEE HEE, I JUST LOVE TO TERRIFY STRANGERS, DEAR. WELCOME TO CASTLE FERNLIK. I'M KINDLY MRS. DOBBINS, BATTY OLE HOUSEKEEPER.

I CAN'T HELP BUT FEEL THAT THERE'S SOMETHING... EERIE HERE. BUT MAYBE THIS IS MY CHANCE FOR HAPPINESS — TUTORING SIR LANCE'S NIECE, ESMEÉ. WATCHING HER GROW INTO GENTEEL WOMANHOOD. I SEE PERHAPS SOME JOY... I SEE SIR LANCE... I... SHIT! I SEE A PIMPLE! RIGHT ON THE TIP OF MY...

WHUPP!

ONLY THE MASTER, SIR LANCE FERNLIK, ACTING UP A BIT. GOT A RIGHT GRAND SPARK O' TEMPER, HE HAS !

MAY I PRESENT SIR LANCE FERNLIK, ESQ.

HIYA, KID.

PLAIN LIL' THING, AREN'T YOU...

BOING!!

THROB

HIS VOICE! THOSE EYE LASHES! THOSE ...AHEM... LIMBS!!

THE DAYS PASSED SWIFTLY. INSTRUCTING ESMEE... THEN PETER RABBIT SAID...

¡PENDEJO! FILS D'UN COCHON!

OBSERVING HOW SIR LANCE OVERSAW HIS VAST HOLDINGS... EMPLOYEES...

FORGET TO WATER THE FERNS, WILL YA?!!

BREAD CRUMBS? HOW DARE YOU MENTION THAT TO MY FACE! YOU STUPID NIT!!

SORRY! SORRY! SORRY! SORRY!

HE'S NEVER BEEN THE SAME SINCE HIS FIRST WIFE DIED. FELL OFF THE SEA CLIFF, SHE DID. WITH THE FAMILY'S TREASURE IN HER ARMS — CHEST FILLED WITH ANCIENT JEWELS. OF COURSE, SOME SAYS IT WAS HIM THAT DONE HER IN — SEEING AS THEY NEVER FOUND HER BODY, DEAR.

MERDE.

AND YET THERE WERE QUIET TIMES, TOO.

THEN I FORECLOSED ON THE BUGGERS...

LET'S JUST SEE WHAT YOU LOOK LIKE WITHOUT THOSE OLE FAT WINDOWPANES...

NO! WAIT! PLEASE...

WHY, YOU'RE JOAN FONTAINE!! UH... I MEAN.. YOU'RE BEAUTIFUL!

THEN I KNEW WHAT ECSTASY MEANT

SMOOCH

THROB THROB

CONTINUED

217

1973

LEE MARRS

1975

MIRA FALARDEAU

1982

AREND VAN DAM

ERNEST
HEMINGWAY
MEMORIAL
BEACH

NO
MALE BONDING
ALLOWED

1978

RICHARD FIALA

1982   SKIP MORROW

ca. 1958   TON SMITS

221

1963

DON MARTIN

1975   LARRY KATZMAN

"You flunked arithmetic."

1946   J. R. WILLIAMS

WE'VE GOT TO DEPROGRAM JUNIOR—HE'S RUN OFF AND JOINED THE PRESBYTERIANS...

1978   MIKE PETERS

223

WINSOR McCAY

JAMES THURBER

"Have you seen my pistol, honey-bun?"

1961   SINÉ

1970   WILLIAM STEIG

CATHY

1982   CATHY GUISEWITE

1980   WILLIAM HAEFELI

1982

MARIAN LYDBROOKE

1964   MARVIN TANNENBERG

*"Of course, there's no such thing as a really bad boy—but now and then
you do get a mean, lousy, rotten kid."*

SKIPPY

1938   PERCY CROSBY

MARY PETTY

"Rubbish! Lots of children are unwanted. Your father and I didn't want you."

NOSTALGIA

CLAIRE BRETÉCHER

1981   RICHARD KIRKMAN

"It's so you can find out what's happening on the local level."

1980   BRUCE COCHRAN

"Dinner's ready, you asshole."

GEORGE BOOTH

NICOLE HOLLANDER

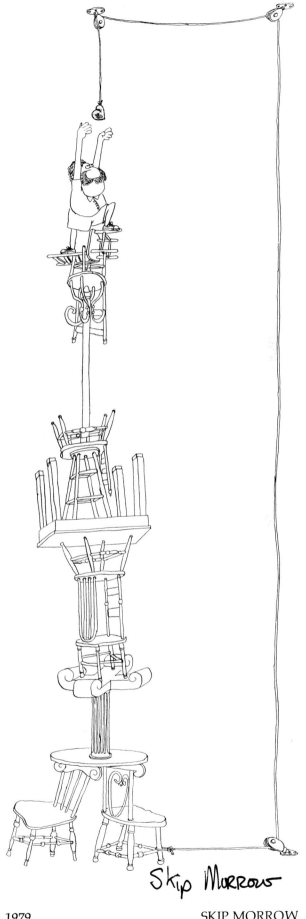

1979   SKIP MORROW

1981   ROBERT ZIMMERMAN

"Myrtle, I just found out we're New Wave."

    WILLIAM HAMILTON

"When I fell in love with you, suddenly your eyes didn't seem close together. Now they seem close together again."

1966   JOHN GLASHAN

JAMES STEVENSON

"Well, here it is, honey. The bottom line."

1978

MICHAEL C. WITTE

ONE GOOD TERN DESERVES ANOTHER

Index of Contributing Artists

ACKNOWLEDGMENTS

The editors, Cartoonists Guild and Crown Publishers wish to express their deepest thanks to all the artists and heirs whose kind cooperation has helped in the creation of *Drawn Together: Relationships Lampooned, Harpooned & Cartooned.*

Special appreciation goes to Renée D. Pennington for her informed, consistent and energetic administrative and editorial assistance from the outset of this project.

The development of this collection owes much to the generous, knowledgeable counsel of cartoonist Marvin Tannenberg, first president of the Cartoonists Guild.

We also want to thank Avis Lang Rosenberg for the information and advice she provided, particularly regarding the cartoonists participating in the international cartoon and comic art exhibition *Pork Roasts: 250 Feminist Cartoons*, of which she was organizer and curator. Our warm appreciation as well to Jill Frisch and her associates in the Rights and Permissions Department of *The New Yorker* for their invaluable assistance.

We are indebted to the following copyright owners for permission to reprint cartoons owned by them:

Cartoons © 1963 and 1971 E. C. Publications, Inc. Cartoons © 1978 and 1980 by Richard Fiala and Charles Ortleb. First published in *Christopher Street* magazine. Cartoon © 1981 Hearst Corp. First published in *Cosmopolitan* magazine. Cartoons © 1982 Holt, Rinehart & Winston. From *The Official I Hate Love Book.* Cartoons © I. H. T. Corporation. Cartoons © 1918, 1919 and 1930 King Features Syndicate. Cartoons © 1944. By permission of Bill Mauldin and Wil-Jo Associates, Inc. Cartoon © 1980 Medical Economics Company, Inc., Oradell, N.J. 07649. Cartoons © 1939, 1946 and 1953 Newspaper Enterprise Association.

Cartoons copyrighted by The New Yorker Magazine, Inc. are indicated throughout the book.

Cartoon © 1980 O'Quinn Studios, Inc. First published in *Fangoria* magazine. Cartoon © 1980 *Punch.* Cartoons © 1968, 1969 and 1970 William Steig. From *Male/Female*, Farrar, Straus & Giroux, Inc. Reprinted by permission. Cartoons © 1976 and 1977 G. B. Trudeau and Universal Press Syndicate. First published in *Doonesbury* syndicated strip by G. B. Trudeau. Cartoons © 1982 United Feature Syndicate, Inc. First published in *Marmaduke* syndicated panel by Brad Anderson. Cartoons © 1980 and 1981 United Feature Syndicate. First published in *Peanuts* syndicated strip by Charles M. Schulz. Cartoon © 1978 United Feature Syndicate. First published in *Wee Pals* syndicated strip by Morrie Turner. Cartoons © 1982 Universal Press Syndicate. First published in *Cathy* syndicated strip by Cathy Guisewite. Cartoons © 1980 and 1981 Universal Press Syndicate. First published in *For Better or For Worse* syndicated strip by Lynn Johnston. Cartoon © 1980 Tom Wolfe. From *In Our Time*, Farrar, Straus & Giroux, Inc. Reprinted by permission.

We particularly want to acknowledge the following heirs of fourteen great cartoonists for their assistance in making many wonderful drawings available to us: Patricia Arno Maxwell, Frances M. Terry (Sam Cobean), Joan Crosby Tibbetts, George W. George (Rube Goldberg), Mrs. John Held, Jr., Selby Kelly, Barbara Rea Renwick, Jane C. Ruge, Lidwien Smits-Zoetmulder, Anna Soglow, Clara Gee Stamaty, Maxine Taylor Hermansader, Helen W. Thurber and David A. Williams (Gluyas Williams). Our book is so much the richer for the inclusion of this body of classic work.

Our sincere thanks go to the following artists who are copyright owners of one or more original drawings published for the first time in this collection: Alan Baral, M. K. Brown, Richard Codor, Frank Collyer, Michael Dater, Don Dougherty, Mort Drucker, Jan Eliot, Jerzy Flisak, Walter Gallup, Pearl Hill, Richard Kirkman, Mike Kreffel, Dave Lester, Marian Lydbrooke, Heather McAdams, Howard Margulies, Roland Michaud, Skip Morrow, Michael Siporin, Jessica Stanley, John Troy and Arend Van Dam.

Grateful acknowledgment is also made to the following publications in whose pages or through whose auspices many of the cartoons reprinted in this book first appeared: *Aftershock, Audubon, The Bee Hive,* Cartoonists & Writers Syndicate, *Chicago, Cultural Correspondence, Dayton Daily News, De Zwijger,* The Dial Press, *Diversion,* E. P. Dutton, Editions Albin Michel, Editions Denoël, *Esquire, Express, Family Advocate, Family Circle, Field and Stream,* Field Newspaper Syndicate, Fireside Press/Simon & Schuster, *Good Housekeeping, Harvey,* Hyperion Press, Inc., *Ladies' Home Journal, Le Jour, Los Angeles Herald-Examiner,* LNS News Service, *Mainmise, Mother Jones, National Enquirer, National Lampoon, New Woman, The New York Review of Books, The New York Times,* The New York Times Special Features, *Oui, Pão Com Manteiga, Parade, Perspectives, Phi Delta Kappan, Prairie State Blues,* Prentice-Hall, G. P. Putnam's Sons, *Raw,* The Real Comet Press, St. Martin's Press, *San Francisco, Skunk Piss, Sourcream, Szpilki,* Viking-Penguin Books, *The Wall Street Journal* and Windmill Press. In some of these instances, drawings from more than one artist are included in this collection. In every case, the artist, as copyright holder, has granted the necessary permission, for which we are most grateful.

Great care has been taken to trace the ownership of every cartoon selected and to make full acknowledgment for its use. If any permissions are omitted through error, necessary apologies and credits will be made.